SHOOGLIES 2

by

GEORGE LANE

222242.J.V. SQUARE AND WAR MEMORIAL, RUTHERGLEN. (7)

Little remains today of Rutherglen's west end. Most of the buildings visible in this picture have gone to make way for road improvements. The War Memorial has been resited.

© 1992 George Lane
First Published in the United Kingdom, 1992
By Richard Stenlake, 1 Overdale Street, Langside, Glasgow G42 9PZ
Tel: 041 632 2304

ISBN 1-872074-18-9

Tram no.750 heads north on the George V Bridge while an ex-Caledonian Railway locomotive hauls a commuter train into Central Station sometime in the mid 1920s.

FOREWORD

There may not have been quite enough technical information to satisfy the tram historians in my first volume of 'The Shooglies', but it was otherwise very well received. It has also done wonders for my popularity at "the dancing"! But, of course, my fame has not spread everywhere. One member of the public picked up the book in my presence and asked "Whereabouts in Glasgow is George Lane anyway? Is it off George Square?"

In response to the many requests, not least of all from Summerlee where I can still be seen driving a "shoogly" some days, I have compiled another nostalgic album of old Glasgow. I hope you enjoy it as much as I have enjoyed putting it together.

George Lane, September 1992.

Tram 370 passes along Dumbarton Road on its way to Dalmarnock past some of the buildings destroyed in the Clydebank blitz.

A busy Union Street in the early 1920s at the junction with Argyle and Jamaica Streets. 571 heads south towards Ibrox, 256 is on its way to Riddrie, while the other tram (whose number is partially obscured by the motorcyclist) is destined for Kirklee.

A busy scene on Jamaica Bridge, with the first of the Coronation Trams (no. 1141) following two standard trams. Part of the rail bridge was removed in the 1960s as rail services declined and it was no longer required.

RENFIELD STREET FROM WEST GEORGE STREET, GLASGOW. A.8229.

The Paramount Cinema on Renfield Street is one of the few cinemas left in Glasgow city centre and has been converted to a multi-screen complex. Just above it can be seen the now-defunct Regent Cinema and the YMCA building.

A standard tram makes its way to Whiteinch past the old Caledonian Railway low level station at Glasgow Cross. The site of this station is now just paved over. The railway line was constructed in 1898.

Argyle Street, Glasgow

This part of Argyle Street is now pedestrianised. Woolworth's has now gone from the city centre but I remember going there as a child with my parents. At Christmas we went to see Santa Claus and for 6d he would slide a present down a chute from his seat in the grotto.

St. George's Cross has been extensively re-developed to make way for the M8 motorway and its associated feeder links. Only the bank building remains today. Most of the tenements have been replaced by modern housing and there are no public toilets here now. The Empress Cinema was part of the Green's Playhouse chain.

Woodlands Road and College of Domestic Science, Glasgow.

Tram No.24 heads down an empty Woodlands Road on its way to its terminus at the University. The College of Domestic Science has become Queens College.

Seamore Street at Maryhill Road was a tram terminus with a passing loop. The tram on the right is heading for Maryhill, while the other is going to Maitland Street. The buildings in the background have been refurbished but the fountain is long gone.

Balgray Hill, Springburn, Glasgow

Only the Barclay Street tenement at the hilltop remains as most of these buildings have been demolished to make way for the dual carriageway to Bishopbriggs. Quin's Balgray Hill entrance had a small bar and a games room. In later years there was a tram shelter in front of Quin's.

RELIABLE ⚭ SERIES 70.

MAIN STREET, BISHOPBRIGGS, GLASGOW.

Tram No. 976 sits at the Bishopbriggs terminus. Its route was to Rouken Glen. The terminus was moved to Kenmure Street due to the amount of vehicles using Kirkintilloch Road.

Main Street, Baillieston circa 1912. In the distance can be seen a tram on its way to Airdrie. The tenements on the right also housed the Co-op.

A Coronation Tram picks up passengers at the Maukinfauld Road stop in Tollcross before heading to Paisley Cross.

983/12.   EASTMUIR. SHETTLESTON.

An open top tram is about to pass Shettleston Academy gates sometime around 1910.

A small boy picks up his flattened penny off the tram lines at Shettleston Cross while Tram No.567 picks up passengers before travelling to Ibrox.

Parkhead Cross is still recognisable today but is much busier. A control tower for the tram points was built where the toilets are located in this pre First World War view.

ALEXANDRA PARADE LOOKING EAST.

Sent by a prison warder from Nottingham (presumably on a visit to Barlinnie) the message on the back of this 1917 postcard reads "Dear Laurie, you will see by this postcard where I am today on escort duty again fetching a poor old boy out of prison for Draft tomorrow, goodbye, Dan"

What a wonderful photo this is of Canning Street (now London Road) as seen from Bridgeton Cross. It must date from around 1908 or thenabouts. Tram 1000 is about to turn to our left on its journey to Cambuslang. The tram which we can see side on is a converted horse tram going to Springburn.

Bridgeton Cross, Glasgow

939 is about to turn onto London Road en route to Alexandra Park. If Glasgow brings back the trams, this route will need changing as where the tram is standing has now been pedestrianised.

This view shows Great Eastern Road at Camlachie. Now renamed Gallowgate, this area looks totally different today. Most of the buildings have gone.

DUKE STREET, GLASGOW.

Duke Street at Belgrove Street. One of the tenements on the right has now been demolished. The policeman on points duty had a much easier life when this photograph was taken.

Crownpoint Sports Ground is now where the buildings on the right are located. All of the other buildings have also been demolished in the re-development of this area of the Gallowgate. The tram is passing Whitevale Cross before heading west along the Gallowgate towards town.

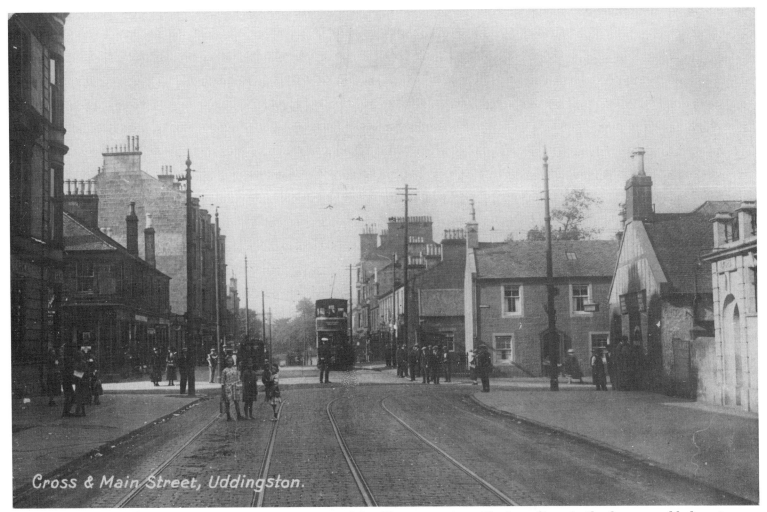

Cross & Main Street, Uddingston.

Uddingston Cross. This was the southern terminus of the Glasgow system. The tram lines in the foreground belong to the Lanarkshire Tramway. Passengers arriving on the Glasgow trams from as far away as Paisley or Clydebank could continue their journey on the Lanarkshire system as far as Larkhall or Wishaw.

JV 58925

The barrow boy has just enough time to get out of the way of Tram No.373 which is heading west to Stobcross Ferry. Cambuslang's main street has changed totally in the last thirty years. When the road was widened, all of the buildings on the left were demolished and new housing and shops built further back from the road.

The inevitable group of children pose for the photographer at Rosslyn Terrace, Stonelaw Road, Rutherglen. The nanny has just passed Rutherglen Hospital on the left.

Car Terminus, Mount Florida.

Just down the road from Hampden Park, this scene has hardly changed since this view was taken in the 1920s. Three tram services terminated here.

Kinning Park Co-operative Society owned the building on the left. I used to go there as a wee boy to get my mother's messages and was fascinated by the little cash containers whizzing about on wires overhead! I can still also to this day remember my mother's co-op divi number! The tram is just passing Jamieson Street on its way along Cathcart Road to Mount Florida Tram Terminus.

CATHCART ROAD FROM DIXON HALL, CROSSHILL, GLASGOW.

E 02808

Outside Dixon Hall (another dancing venue) was the Govanhill terminus. This consisted of a passing loop. Car No.8 is heading for Paisley Road Toll while Tram No. 982 is passing on its way to the Mount Florida terminus.

916 for Clarkston makes its way for us here at the gates of Queen's Park. During the war, my pals and I used to walk up and down 'the Burma Road' - our name for this bit of Victoria Road - trying to "get a lumber".

Pollokshaws Road, Shawlands, Glasgow.

It takes a second or two to place this view exactly (Pollokshaws Road at Minard Road) but actually it still looks much the same today. Maybe it just isn't so easy to recognise without all the snarled up buses and traffic! Just outside the picture, to the left, was another of my dancing haunts The Top Hat. Now that I have retired I'm going to the dancing again!

Entrance to Rouken Glen

A childhood treat for my sister and I was for our parents to take us a hurl in the caur to Rouken Glen. At Easter we rolled our eggs down the hills there. Later, when we were teenagers, we went for boat rides on the loch.

The two trams are passing what is now the area underneath the Kingston Bridge. On the left is the Kingston Library, which is now a refuge for down and outs. Beside it was the Rolls Royce Social Club.

Waiting in the passing loop at Paisley Road Toll is Tram No.365 before it heads off to Riddrie. Behind it is Ogg Brothers' shop which is now a restaurant.

Fairfield's offices are still there in Govan Road but the tenements on the right are long gone and have been replaced by new houses.

Linthouse, Glasgow

Linthouse, Govan. Part of the building on the right has been demolished to make way for the entrance to the Clyde Tunnel. The unusual bracket at the top of the pole on the right was used for lifting the tram lines higher so that high loads could make their way to the docks. Tram No. 809 is trundling along to the Shieldhall terminus.

Tram No. 1093 was one of a series of cars built specially for the route to Paisley West but a series of derailments caused their transfer to the route from Argyle Street to Dalmuir. The tram on the left is on its way to Airdrie.

A policeman directs traffic and lets a car out in front of an ex-Paisley & District tram No.1057 which is heading to Potterhill. This junction is controlled by traffic lights today.

WAR MEMORIAL, HAIRST STREET, RENFREW

A Coronation Tram is about to pass Renfrew Town Hall on its way to Renfrew Ferry. On the right today there is a shopping mall and the war memorial has become part of a roundabout.

Paisley & District Tram No.16 passes Houston Square, Johnstone on its way to Renfrew Ferry.

Another Paisley tram passes Cowan Park Gates on Darnley Road, Barrhead on its way to Rouken Glen.

GT WESTERN ROAD KELVIN BRIDGE GLASGOW

It seems a pity that these beautiful ornamental traction poles up the middle of the road have gone. Also away from this view - the tenement on the left. Tram 962 passes it on its way to Dennistoun.

Tram No. 906 passes under the beautiful Victorian cast iron traction poles at Kelvinside on its way east towards Parkhead.

ANNIESLAND CROSS LOOKING EAST, GLASGOW. A.4140.

Photographed in 1936, there are four trams visible in this view of Anniesland Cross. Again, major alterations to the road layout have taken place here as the amount of traffic has increased greatly since World War Two.

Trams Nos. 741 and 845 sit at the Hyndland terminus. 741 will continue onto Jordanhill while 645 will be heading to Langside.

Clarence Drive, Hyndland

Car 362 descends a calmer, quieter Clarence Drive on its way to Jordanhill. I tried to take a picture from the same spot - I like to do 'now and then' comparisons - the traffic made it so dangerous I was almost part of the then myself!

In recent years, the Kelvin Hall has become the Museum of Transport. No doubt some of the trams in there must have passed it during their working lives. Here 327 going to Cambuslang passes an Albion Venturer going to Knightswood.

DUMBARTON ROAD, PARTICK

The tram is just about to pass under the bridge at Partick West railway station on the route to Dalmuir. The railway bridge has now gone and there is now a children's playground where the railway tracks were behind the tenements. The buildings here have been refurbished and stonecleaned.

A line of trams is led by Tram No. 122 on its way along Dumbarton Road to Scotstoun. Merkland Street (now Partick) Underground Station is just around the corner on the right.

This looks west along Dumbarton Road from Partick towards Whiteinch where the tram on our left will terminate. The tram on the right is being held up on its eastbound journey by a clutter of horses and carts. A far cry from today now that a motorway system dominates this area.

The low railway bridges on Kilbowie Road necessitated having single deck trams. Ex-Paisley & District trams were cut down and used specifically for this service. A group of workers has obviously just got off the tram and are heading off to work at John Browns. 1012 is waiting before heading back north to Duntocher.